CANARY THREADS

THE STORY OF 50 NORWICH CITY SHIRTS

KEVIN GOODINGS

All profits to the Norwich City
Community Sports Foundation

Published in Great Britain in 2024 by
Kevin Goodings

Copyright © Kevin Goodings, 2024

All rights reserved; no part of this publication may be reproduced, stored in a retrieval system, or transmitted, in any form or by any means, electronic, mechanical, photocopying, recording or otherwise, without the prior written permission of the publisher. Nor be circulated in any form of binding or cover other than that in which it is published and a similar condition including this condition being imposed on the subsequent purchaser.

For licensing requests, please contact the author at
hello@ontheballcity.co.uk.

The author's rights are fully asserted. The right of Kevin Goodings to be identified as the author of this work has been asserted in accordance with the Copyright, Designs and Patents Act 1988

A CIP Catalogue of this book is available from
the British Library

ISBN: 978-1-3999-9220-6

Photography by Luke Witcomb –
www.lukewitcombphotography.com

Cover design and typeset by
www.chandlerbookdesign.com

Printed in Great Britain by
Short Run Press Ltd.

*For RG who spent so much time taking me
to so many games and
DG who waited patiently at home
for us to get back.*

CONTENTS

Introduction		1
1965/66	Ron Davies	5
1971/72	Division 2 Champions	7
1972/73	First Division Canaries	9
1972/73	New Club Crest	11
1972/73	League Cup Final	13
1973/74	Kevin Keelan	17
1974/75	Promotion to Division 1	19
1974/75	League Cup Final	21
1976/77	The Admiral Years – Home	23
1977/78	The Admiral Years – Away	27
1978/79	Martin Peters Testimonial	29
1979/80	The Admiral Years – Goalkeeper	31
1981/82	Martin O'Neill	33
1983/84	Poll Withey Windows	35
1984/85	Milk Cup Final	37
1985/86	Division 2 Champions	39
1986/87	Top 5 City	41
1988/89	FA Cup Semi-Final	43
1991/92	Bryan Gunn	45
1991/92	FA Cup Semi-Final	47
1992/93	Ian Crook	49
1993/94	Mark Robins (Home)	51
1993/94	Mark Robins (Away)	53

1993/94	Vitesse Arnhem	55
1993/94	Bayern Munich	57
1994/95	Premier League Relegation	59
1995/96	On Loan to the Endsleigh League	61
2001/02	Marc Libbra	63
2001/02	Division 1 Play-Off Semi-Final	65
2001/02	Division 1 Play-Off Final	67
2002/03	Centenary Season	69
2003/04	Division 1 Champions	71
2004/05	Darren Huckerby	73
2005/06	Craig Fleming	75
2007/08	XX Special Edition	77
2008/09	Celebrating the '59ers	79
2009/10	Division 1 Champions	81
2010/11	Promoted to the Premier League	83
2012/13	Grant Holt's Last Game	85
2012/13	FA Youth Cup Winners	87
2014/15	Championship Play-Off Final	89
2015/16	80 years at Carrow Road	91
2017/18	James Maddison	93
2018/19	Champions at Villa Park	95
2019/20	FA Cup Quarter-Final	97
2020/21	To the Fans	99
2020/21	Teemu Pukki	101
2020/21	Champions at Oakwell	103
2022/23	Gabriel Sara	105
2023/24	Norwich City 1 Ipswich Town 0	107

Appendix   109

   ABOUT THE AUTHOR
   BILLY POINTER
   NORWICH CITY COMMUNITY SPORTS FOUNDATION

Off to the match with my Dad and brother in 1979.

Introduction

I am a Norwich fan because they were my Dad's team. There was never any discussion about supporting a different club and it wasn't long before we were making regular trips to Carrow Road together.

My Dad worked most weekends so the games we went to in the beginning were midweek matches under the floodlights. It's why I still prefer night games. They remind me of the times I went with him and my younger brother.

My first game was in 1978 when Admiral supplied the Norwich kit. Unlike today, there were no sponsor logos on the front or back. No sleeve patches. No player names either, just simple stitched numbers from 1 to 12. The shirts looked great.

Admiral's designs kick-started the replica kit market in the '70s. With some effort over many months, I eventually saved enough of my pocket money to buy my own replica kit from the Pilch store that was on the corner of Orford Place in the centre of Norwich. I even got a green number 11 which my mum had to add to the back of the shirt so I could pretend to be Martin Peters. It was the start of a long-lasting love of football shirts; especially those that came in Canary yellow.

As much as I loved my replica strip, I knew it was different from the ones actually worn by my heroes. The replica had a yellow Admiral logo not a white one. The logo and club badge were simple transfers whilst the player's shirts had proper stitched ones. I often wondered how you could get hold of a "real" Norwich shirt.

Time passes to the moment in 1993 when Bryan Gunn organised a charity auction of football shirts which included Ian Crook's number 7. I had never seen an event like it. A friend's wedding meant I couldn't go to the auction but I sent my brother instead with strict

Wembley, 2015

instructions to buy that shirt whatever the price. I was delighted to pick-up a voicemail later that evening where he shared news that he had got the last, winning bid on it. That shirt became my first "real" Norwich shirt.

I paid more attention to auctions and I found other City shirts. I picked-up the number 7 from the 1973 League Cup final from a Mullock Madely auction soon after. Next, the number 10 from the 1989 FA Cup Semi-Final was sold by Radio Broadland. Getting that meant I suddenly had a collection.

Eventually, an original Admiral number 11 Norwich shirt came up for sale. I could barely breathe when I saw it as it would have been worn by Martin Peters. It is my most treasured shirt because it's got such a connection to those first trips to Carrow Road with my Dad from decades ago.

Over the years, I have continued to pick-up "real" Norwich City shirts and I have them listed on my website at ontheballcity.co.uk. Today, it's relatively easy to acquire match worn or player issue shirts. Players regularly throw them into the crowd after every game and, if you have the funds, clubs run their own auctions selling hundreds over a season. You can also find lots of shirts online and at sports memorabilia auctions too.

Match worn and player issue shirts have become very collectable and potentially a good investment as prices only seem to increase as interest levels rise. Who would have thought Maradona's Hand of God shirt from 1986 would sell for over £7m years later?

A large community of collectors has formed including others that share my particular passion for those special yellow and green Norwich ones.

Books have been published featuring collections of shirts for England, Manchester City, West Ham, Leeds and others. All of the biggest clubs in the country it seems but somehow Norwich City has been missed.

To correct this, I felt it was time for this book to be produced so that those special yellow shirts can take their place alongside the rest. We may not have won as many titles and trophies as some other clubs but we've always had the best, most unique kit colours in all of England.

The intention was to tell the story of 50 Norwich City shirts. Those included are connected to great moments in the club's history or to players that became legends or just great designs that I particularly like. They are all threads in the colourful story of the Canaries.

I would like to thank Billy Pointer and Wes Hoolahan for supporting this book and allowing their shirts to be featured alongside some from my own collection. Also, David 'Spud' Thornhill for his solid fact checking of each of the stories.

All profits from the sale of this book will go to the excellent Norwich City Community Sports Foundation. A wonderful organisation that makes a positive difference locally to the lives of so many.

OTBC

My Dad and my son at Carrow Road in 2024

1965
1966

4 **1965/66** RON DAVIES

1965/66 Ron Davies

This is the oldest Norwich City shirt I have found so far. It was made by Umbro and the design was used for 8 seasons between 1962/63 and 1968/69.

This particular shirt was worn by Ron Davies. He joined from Luton Town and played 126 games scoring 66 goals for the Canaries between 1963 and 1966. At the time, City were a mid-table side in Division 2.

His success earned him a move to Southampton and a step up to the First Division. He went on to score 134 goals in 240 games for the Saints before further spells at Portsmouth and Manchester United.

This shirt was given to a young City fan who was utterly distraught when he left. Ron was a hero to many more Canary fans. Years later, when I was fortunate enough to become the shirt's current custodian, my father-in-law, a tough old Norfolk builder, was moved to tears when he saw it. It instantly brought back memories of his own meeting with Ron at an awards ceremony when he was a kid.

1971
1972

6 **1971/72** DIVISION 2 CHAMPIONS

1971/72 Division 2 Champions

The Canaries joined Division 3 of the Football League in 1920/21. They won promotion to Division 2 in 1933/34 and survived for 5 seasons before relegation in 1938/39. It would take until the 1959/60 season for the club to return to the 2nd Division where they established themselves. The 1971/72 season was their 12th consecutive season at this level. It would prove historic as they finally achieved promotion to the 1st Division for the first time ever.

Under manager Ron Saunders, the Canaries would finish top of the Division 2 table with 57 points from 42 games; 1 point ahead of Birmingham City and 2 in front of Millwall. Promotion was won at Orient on 24 April 1972 with a 2-1 win in front of 15,530 fans. The title was secured a few days later at Watford.

This shirt was worn by Norfolk-born Max Briggs who made a total of 170 appearances between 1968 and 1974.

City wore these Umbro styled shirts for 3 seasons from 1969/70 to 1971/72. They were accompanied by black shorts until those were replaced with green ones for the 1971/72 season. Apart from a couple "all yellow" kit seasons in the late 90's, City have worn green shorts to the present day.

1972
1973

8 **1972/73** FIRST DIVISION CANAFIES

1972/73 First Division Canaries

The Canaries first ever game in Division One was against Everton at Carrow Road on 12 August 1972. The 1-1 draw was watched by 25,851. Jimmy Bone scored the first ever Norwich City goal at this level.

Their first away game was even better. A 2-1 win at Ipswich Town on 15th August 1972 in front of 29,828 fans. Jimmy Bone scored again as did Terry Anderson.

For the first 10 games of the season, City would wear plain yellow Canary shirts with green trim around the collar and sleeves but no club crest as it was being re-designed. This had been prompted by Chairman Geoffrey Watling who was keen to have a new crest that could be protected by copyright.

1972
1973

10 **1972/73** NEW CLUB CREST

1972/73 New Club Crest

The new club crest was finally added to the Norwich shirts on 16 September 1972 for the game at West Ham United.

The new badge was designed by local architect Andrew Anderson. He earnt just £10 for his winning design in a competition run by the Eastern Evening News and judged by his former grammar school art master!

His design would go on to appear on the Canaries shirts for 50 years until it was updated again in 2022.

City would use this style of shirt with green shorts for two seasons. Oddly, in this first Division 1 season, the Canaries would sometimes wear green rather than yellow socks for some of their games.

1972
1973

12   1972/73 LEAGUE CUP FINAL

1972/73 League Cup Final

As well as playing in Division One for the first time, the Canaries also made their first ever appearance at Wembley for the League Cup final on 3 March 1973. They had beaten Leicester City, Hull City, Stockport County, Arsenal and Chelsea on their way to the final.

A crowd of 100,000 watched a disappointing 1-0 defeat to Tottenham Hotspur with Ralph Coates getting the winner after 72 minutes. Doug Livermore wore the number 7 shirt in the Norwich team.

As well as the "Wembley 1973" text, the club badge was altered with the League Cup trophy replacing the usual lion and castle in the left-hand corner. The tracksuit top was worn as the teams walked out onto the pitch. This also included the one-off League Cup final badge and text.

14 1972/73 LEAGUE CUP FINAL

1973
1974

16   1973/74 KEVIN KEELAN

1973/74 Kevin Keelan

This is Kevin Keelan's goalkeeper's shirt; given to a fan at the end of a very difficult second season in Division 1. Geoffrey Watling stepped down as Chairman and was succeeded by Sir Authur South on 30 August 1973. Ron Saunders resigned after a 3-1 home defeat to Everton on 17 November 1973 and was replaced by John Bond. The Canaries won just 7 league matches all season and finished bottom of the final league table with 29 points.

Keelan played in all 42 league games that season and won his second Player of the Year award. I don't think his club record 673 appearances accrued over 17 years will ever be beaten. He was awarded a testimonial match in 1974 against Ipswich Town and a retirement benefit game against an All Star XI in 1980.

Signed from Wrexham for £6,500, Keelan is an undoubted club legend as well as inaugural member of the Hall of Fame. This was created in the 2002/03 centenary season to honour those that had made the greatest contribution to the club in its long history both on and off the pitch.

1974
1975

18   **1974/75** PROMOTION TO DIVISION 1

1974/75 Promotion to Division 1

Under John Bond's management, the Canaries returned to Division One at the first attempt in 1974/75.

They finished third in the final Division Two table with 53 points; behind Manchester United and Aston Villa but 2 points ahead of Sunderland. They also reached the League Cup final.

Umbro continued to supply the Norwich kit and this design was worn for 2 seasons.

The style of the previous shirts was updated with minor changes - the round neck was out and replaced with stylish green collars instead. The Umbro logo was printed on the shirt and green colour numbers were stitched on the back.

1974
1975

20 1974/75 LEAGUE CUP FINAL

1974/75 League Cup Final

The Canaries returned to Wembley for the second time in three years for the League Cup Final.

This time they had beaten Bolton Wanderers, West Bromwich Albion, Sheffield United, Ipswich Town and Manchester United to win through to play Aston Villa on 1 March 1975.

100,000 watched another disappointing City performance as Villa triumphed 1-0. Ray Graydon netted on the rebound after Kevin Keelan had saved his late penalty.

For the match, Tony Powell wore number 11. This shirt features the same amended club badge as used in the 1973 final but with "Wembley 1975" wording underneath. Tony played for Norwich between 1974 and 1981. He was the Player of the Season in 1978/79.

1976
1977

22   **1976/77** THE ADMIRAL YEARS – HOME

1976/77 The Admiral Years – Home

This classic Norwich City shirt features a sewn-on Admiral logo and club badge with a stitched number 11 on the back.

The Canaries wore Admiral designed kits for 5 seasons, all in Division 1, from 1976/77 to 1980/81 finishing 16th, 13th, 16th, 12th and then 20th respectively.

City were an entertaining team under manager John Bond but he left on 11 October 1980 to join Manchester City and led them to the centenary FA Cup final. Ken Brown took over but wasn't able to save the Canaries from relegation. Ultimately, he would go on to become one of the most successful City managers in his own right.

Also shown here is an original Admiral tracksuit supplied to the Canaries alongside the playing strip. Its design continues to be popular to the present day with fans wearing retro versions of this tracksuit regularly seen at Carrow Road on match day.

1977
1978

26   **1977/78** THE ADMIRAL YEARS – AWAY

1977/78 The Admiral Years – Away

In the 5 seasons that Norwich wore Admiral, they had two different styles for their away shirts.

The first design was all white similar to the Leeds United kit of the time but using green trim instead of blue. I've only ever seen photos of this.

This was replaced by the second design shown here which introduced green sleeves with white admiral logos on a black trim on the shoulders. There is another version of these green and white away shirts that used white admiral logos on green trim.

Unlike the present day, the away kit was only used when the Canaries kit clashed. In reality, that limited its use to pre-season games at Cambridge United and trips to Wolverhampton Wanderers.

1978
1979

28   **1978/79** MARTIN PETERS TESTIMONIAL

1978/79 Martin Peters Testimonial

1966 World Cup winner Martin Peters played 207 games and scored 44 goals for Norwich City between 1975 and 1980.

He signed for just £40,000 from Tottenham Hotspur when he was 31. He won the Player of the Season award in 1975/76 and again in 1976/77.

He was granted a testimonial match which was played on 18 October 1978. Norwich took on the England team from the 1996 World Cup winning 4-2.

This long-sleeve number 6 shirt was worn on the night by Tony Powell and doesn't have the usual club badge. Instead, it was replaced with one-off embroidery of the match details.

1979
1980

30 1979/80 THE ADMIRAL YEARS – GOALKEEPER

1979/80 The Admiral Years – Goalkeeper

This green top would have been worn by City's keepers in the Admiral years such as Kevin Keelan, Roger Hansbury, Clive Baker and Chris Woods.

At the time, the club only received a few strips each year and they saw plenty of action with all of the first team, reserve team and youth team games over the season. The sleeves on this particular shirt have been repaired as they have been torn through from all the use.

Although the green top was used most often in the Admiral years, there was also a red goalkeeper top for the 76/77 season. I have yet to find one of these and can only hope at least one has survived somewhere.

1981
1982

32   1981/82 MARTIN O'NEILL

1981/82 Martin O'Neill

This long-sleeve shirt was worn by Martin O'Neill. He had been signed by Ken Brown along with Dave Watson, Chris Woods and Steve Walford in the second half of the 80/81 season in an unsuccessful attempt at avoiding relegation to Division 2.

At the time, O'Neill was a headline signing for Norwich having won two European Cups, two League Cups and a First Division title with Nottingham Forest. O'Neill moved to Manchester City after the heart breaking 3-2 defeat at home to Leicester City on the last day of the season which confirmed City's relegation.

He returned to Carrow Road in February 1982 and was the driving force behind a late surge that saw the Canaries promoted in third place after winning 14 of their final 21 matches. He left again in 1983 to join Notts County.

O'Neill's final spell at Norwich was as manager in 1995 for just 6 brief months. A disagreement with chairman Robert Chase prompted O'Neill to quit and join Leicester City. He promptly led them to promotion via the Play-Offs before top ten Premier League finishes and two League Cups. You can't help but wonder what would have happened if he had stayed in Norfolk for a bit longer each time he was here.

1983
1984

34   1983/84 POLL WITHEY WINDCWS

1983/84 Poll Withey Windows

Liverpool were the first professional team in England to have a shirt sponsor when they signed a £50,000 deal with Hitachi in 1979.

Initially, clubs were prevented from wearing sponsored shirts in broadcast TV matches but these rules were relaxed for the 1983/84 season. As a result, all the Division 1 clubs ended up with shirt sponsors for that season.

Local company Poll Withey Windows became Norwich City's first shirt sponsor; worn for the first time against Leicester City on 19 October 1983. Their bright red branding can be seen on this white away shirt from that time. They would sponsor the shirts for 3 seasons.

Since then, the front shirt sponsors have included Foster's Lager, Asics, Norwich & Peterborough, Colman's, Digital Phone Company, Proton, Flybe, Aviva, Aviva Community Fund, LeoVegas, Dafabet, Lotus and now Blakely Clothing.

1984
1985

36   1984/85 MILK CUP FINAL

1984/85 Milk Cup Final

Sunday 24 March 1985 will forever be remembered in the Norwich City history books as the day the Canaries won the Milk Cup. It was their first victory at Wembley after defeats in the League Cup finals of 1973 and 1975.

City had beaten Preston North End, Aldershot, Notts County, Grimsby Town and most enjoyably Ipswich Town to reach the final.

On the day, the best team won. Asa Hartford's shot, deflected off Sunderland's Gordon Chisholm early in the second half, was enough to see the Canaries to a 1-0 win. Sunderland's best chance came shortly after the goal. Clive Walker missed a penalty after Dennis Van Wyk's very obvious handball.

This is Peter Mendham's shirt from the final. It was one of just 15 specially made with the "Milk Cup Final 1985" wording printed above the crest for the game. The shirt also features the distinctive Hummel chevrons on the shoulders and the side.

1985
1986

38   1985/86 DIVISION 2 CHAMPIONS

1985/86 Division 2 Champions

The Canaries followed the success of winning the Milk Cup in March with relegation back to the second division in May. Just 3 wins and 8 defeats in their last 13 matches after Wembley.

Coventry City had 3 games left to play, including the champions Everton, after Norwich had finished their season. They duly won them all and City went down, 1 point short of safety.

It was a miserable summer too. On 2 June 1985, UEFA banned all English clubs from competing in Europe after the Heysel stadium tragedy so City missed out after earning a place for winning the Milk Cup.

As it happens, after all this, the 1985/86 season turned out brilliantly with Norwich winning 25 of 42 games to finish as Champions of Division 2 on 84 points; 7 points clear of Charlton Athletic and 8 ahead of Wimbledon.

1986
1987

40 **1986/87** TOP 5 CITY

1986/87 Top 5 City

Manager Ken Brown followed up winning the Milk Cup in 1985 and the 2nd Division title in 1986 by leading the Canaries, at that time, to their highest ever league finish.

This was particularly notable as both Chris Woods and Dave Watson had left in the summer and were replaced by Bryan Gunn and Ian Butterworth. A final 5th place was achieved in a season with memorable away successes at Old Trafford and, on the last day of the season, Highbury. There were excellent home wins against Liverpool, Spurs and Nottingham Forest too.

There was almost another trip to Wembley in the Full Members Cup. City took a last minute lead at Charlton in the semi-final only to concede an even later equaliser and then lose 2-1 in extra-time!

This was the last season the Canaries wore Hummel kits. They provided some of the most distinctive and well-liked designs that Norwich have ever had. It's a shame the partnership wasn't longer or that it's never been renewed since.

1988
1989

42 **1988/89** FA CUP SEMI-FINAL

1988/89 FA Cup Semi-Final

This is Ian Crook's shirt from City's second ever FA Cup Semi-Final on 15 April 1989.

In previous rounds, they had beaten Port Vale 3-1, Sutton United 8-0, Sheffield United 3-2 and West Ham United 3-1 in a replay. The semi-final draw sent them to Villa Park to play Everton.

Norwich had been enjoying a really good season and doing well in the league. They were many people's favourites going into the game. I was confident they would get to Wembley.

However, it was not to be. The Canaries lost a tight game to a horrible goal. Pat Nevin reacted quickest to score following a scramble after Ian Crook accidentally deflected an Everton cross against his own crossbar.

1991
1992

44   1991/92 BRYAN GUNN

1991/92 Bryan Gunn

Bryan Gunn is forever a Norwich City legend and one of the most popular Canaries of recent times.

He made 477 appearances between 1986 and 1998 and was a big part of the team that finished 3rd in the Premier League in 92/93 and the UEFA cup games in the following season. Manchester United came to Carrow Road for his testimonial on 4 November 1996. He had many roles at the club after his playing career finished including a spell as manager.

This shirt is from the 91/92 season when Gunn made 25 appearances before he was injured at Sheffield United on 18 January 1992. Mark Walton took the number 1 shirt for the rest of the season. City finished 18th but there were very decent runs in both cups reaching the League Cup Quarter Final and FA Cup Semi-Final.

1991
1992

46 1991/92 FA CUP SEMI-FINAL

1991/92 FA Cup Semi-Final

The Canaries had really good draws in each round of the 1991/92 FA Cup run.

Barnsley, Millwall and Notts County were comfortably beaten at home. A goalless draw at Southampton in the quarter-final was then followed by a dramatic 2-1 extra time win in the replay at Carrow Road.

The draw matched City with Sunderland at Hillsborough. They were a mid-table 2nd division side. It was City's best ever chance to reach the Wembley final.

Unfortunately, it was a semi-final defeat again. Despite his best efforts beforehand, Robert Fleck was less than 100% fit and would be substituted before the end of the game. City missed good chances before and after Sunderland scored the only goal but just couldn't impose their superior quality on the game.

This is captain Mark Bowen's shirt from the semi-final played on 5 April 1992.

1992
1993

48 1992/93 IAN CROOK

1992/93 Ian Crook

A final day 3-3 draw at Middlesbrough secured a highest ever finish in the first ever Premier League season for City in 1993.

It could have been even better with the Canaries sitting top of the Premier League after beating Aston Villa on 24 March with just 6 games remaining. Ultimately, 3 defeats in those final games saw Norwich drop to 3rd place and finish 12 points behind eventual champions Manchester United.

The season was made even more memorable by the Ribero kit worn by the Canaries which continues to divide opinion to this day. You either love it or you hate it. It's either one of the best Premier League kits ever or one of the worst. The fact is it will always be associated with our most successful league season so far.

This particular shirt was worn by Ian Crook in the final game of that 92/93 season. Ian made over 400 appearances for the Canaries between 1986 and 1997 and was rewarded with a testimonial game against Sparta Rotterdam. He cemented his legend status at the club when he agreed to join Ipswich at the end of the 95/96 season only to re-sign for City. Mike Walker was re-appointed manager and persuaded him to change his mind without ever playing for Town!

1993
1994

50 1993/94 MARK ROBINS (HOME)

1993/94 Mark Robins (Home)

Norwich City's kit manufacturer, Ribero, fell into administration a few months into the 93/94 season. Mitre took over as the club's supplier for the rest of the season. They simply added a Mitre patch over the original Ribero logo to re-brand the kit!

City dropped from 7th to finish 12th in the Premier League after manager Mike Walker resigned and left for Everton in January.

This is Mark Robins' shirt from the 93/94 season. He played 78 times for Norwich and scored 21 goals. He was signed from Manchester United and left for Leicester City. He was the first English player to score a Premier League hat-trick when Norwich won 3-2 at Oldham Athletic on 9 November 1992.

1993
1994

52   1993/94 MARK ROBINS (AWAY)

1993/94 Mark Robins (Away)

The Riberio purple/white away kit used by Norwich for the 92/93 and 93/94 season is almost as iconic as the yellow and green home design.

The away shirt was only ever used in one competitive game - a 2-1 defeat in a League Cup game at Bradford City on 22 September 1993.

It's interesting to note that Mitre didn't bother to add a patch over the Ribero logo on the away kit given its lack of use.

Player squad numbers and names were introduced on shirts in the Premier League for the first time in the 93/94 season.

1993
1994

54 1993/94 VITESSE ARNHEM

1993/94 Vitesse Arnhem

Norwich played their first ever competitive European match on 15 September 1993 at Carrow Road against Vitesse Arnhem in the UEFA cup.

Efan Ekoku scored City's first ever European goal in a 3-0 win with Jeremy Goss and John Polston getting the others. The game was watched by a surprisingly small crowd of just 16,818.

The Canaries were held to a 0-0 draw in the second leg on 29 September 1993.

For this game, City wore their third kit to avoid a clash with the home team's colours. UEFA's restrictions meant the Norwich & Peterborough logo was slightly changed too. Ian Butterworth was number 4 in the City line-up on the night.

1993
1994

56   1993/94 BAYERN MUNICH

1993/94 Bayern Munich

The 3-2 aggregate win over Bayern Munich in the second round of the UEFA Cup has been called the "pinnacle of Norwich City's history". It's certainly one of the many high points. The 2-1 win in Germany on 19 October 1993 was followed by a 1-1 draw at Carrow Road on 3 November 1993.

This number 10 shirt was worn by Ruel Fox in the second leg of the tie and swapped with Bayern's Brazilian right back Jorginho.

The jumbo-sized shirt features the UEFA 1993-94 lettering above and below the club badge and, in comparison to the league shirts, a different print set for the number on the back with no name or sleeve badges.

Ruel Fox was born in Ipswich but played 219 times for Norwich scoring 25 goals. He was exciting to watch and his move to Newcastle United in February 1994 marked the beginning of the end of the great Norwich team that he played in.

1994
1995

58   1994/95 PREMIER LEAGUE RELEGATION

1994/95 Premier League Relegation

The Canaries have made some unusual choices for their away kit over the years but this particular design must rank as one of the most curious.

City used this blue tartan shirt design for two seasons. I still have no idea why Mitre decided to introduce such a strong Scottish influence to the kit or to pick the colours of our local rivals.

This shirt was worn by Mike Milligan in the Premier League for the 94/95 season. Chris Sutton had been sold to Blackburn Rovers before the start of the campaign but City were still in 7th place at Christmas.

Bryan Gunn's broken and dislocated ankle at Nottingham Forest was the catalyst for a collapse in form. One win in the final twenty games. Norwich were relegated as 1 of 4 teams to go down as the Premier League reduced the number of clubs in the top division to 20.

1995
1996

60 1995/96 ON LOAN TO THE ENDSLEIGH LEAGUE

1995/96 On Loan to the Endsleigh League

Martin O'Neill's return as manager in June 1995 massively increased confidence that the Canaries would make an immediate return to the Premier League following a dismal relegation. It prompted the club shop to do a run of "On Loan to the Endsleigh League" t-shirts that proved very popular.

City made a good start but the season declined rapidly when O'Neill resigned in December. He wanted Dean Windass from Hull City. Chairman Robert Chase wouldn't sign him so O'Neill quit and went to Leicester City and got them promoted instead.

The protests that followed from supporters about the poor results and regular sales of the best players eventually led to Robert Chase leaving at the end of the season and Geoffrey Watling bought his shareholding.

2001
2002

62 2001/02 MARC LIBBRA

2001/02 Marc Libbra

Marc Libbra will always be remembered for an incredible Carrow Road debut goal for Norwich. He came on as a substitute for Iwan Roberts with 15 minutes to go against Kevin Keegan's Manchester City on 18 August 2001.

Within 11 seconds he had scored the game's opening goal as he lifted the ball over a Manchester City defender before volleying past Nicky Weaver in the goal. It was the fastest ever debut goal by a Canary. A magical moment of exceptional skill. Paul McVeigh added another to secure a 2-0 home win.

Marc would play just 34 games for the Canaries scoring 7 goals. This match-worn long-sleeve shirt was swapped in an FA Cup game against Chelsea and features the special centenary wording under the club badge.

2001
2002

64 2001/02 DIVISION 1 PLAY-OFF SEMI-FINAL

2001/02 Division 1 Play-Off Semi-Final

Nigel Worthington was the first Norwich City manager to reach the end of season play-offs. It was a significant achievement. Norwich had been relegated from the Premier League in 1994/95 and had finished 16th, 13th, 15th, 9th, 12th and 15th in the 6 seasons that had followed.

City snuck into 6th place on goal difference on the last day of the season with a 2-0 win over 10-man Stockport County.

In the semi-final, they faced Wolverhampton Wanderers. At Carrow Road, the Canaries went behind in the first half but came back strongly to finish as 3-1 winners. Mark Rivers, Paul McVeigh and Malky MacKay got the goals.

Over 27,000 fans, including a sizable away following, watched the return leg at Molineux. It's probably the most intense, hostile atmosphere I've ever experienced. City held out until 12 minutes from time when Robert Green was beaten by Kevin Cooper's long-range shot. Then the pressure really increased but City stood firm to win through to the Cardiff final.

This is Robert Green's shirt from the semi-final.

2001 2002

66   2001/02 DIVISION I PLAY-OFF FINAL

2001/02 Division 1 Play-Off Final

Birmingham City beat Millwall to win through to meet the Canaries in the Division 1 Play-Off final at the Millennium Stadium on 12 May 2002.

It was a great occasion with the atmosphere enhanced by the stadium's closed roof. Watching the game, I felt Norwich played the best but Birmingham had the better chances. We could have won it late at the end of normal time. We might have held on to our lead in extra time. Unfortunately, we didn't and lost 4-2 on penalties.

This shirt was issued to Paul Hayes who was in the travelling squad for the final. It features the one-off match details embroidered above the badge.

Despite the defeat, it has been a terrific season. Reaching the play-offs renewed the interest and levels of support for the Canaries in the years that followed.

2002
2003

68   **2002/03** CENTENARY SEASON

2002/03 Centenary Season

Norwich City celebrated their centenary in the 2002/03 season. To mark the occasion, the club issued a special one-off kit that reflected the very first strip worn by the team in 1902/03. Those original blue and white halves are a very long way from the Canary colours that we all love today.

The centenary kit featured a one-off design for the badge using two Canary birds sitting on a single football; one looking back at the past whilst the other is looking forward to the future. The shirt also included the names of all of the season ticket holders who ordered the shirt in its fabric.

The kit was only used twice: a pre-season centenary friendly against Ajax and a league game at Wolverhampton Wanderers. Both matches were lost 1-0. Nicky Southall made 9 appearances for City during a short loan spell from Bolton Wanderers.

2003
2004

70 2003/04 DIVISION I CHAMPIONS

2003/04 Division 1 Champions

The Canaries ended 9 consecutive seasons of Division One football by winning the title in the 2003/04 season. They finished with 94 points from 46 games; 8 points clear of West Bromwich Albion.

Darren Huckerby's loan and then permanent signing was the trigger for a marvellous season full of entertaining football, great games and wonderful goals.

At Carrow Road, the old South stand was re-developed during the season and formally re-opened for the visit of West Ham United on 21 February 2004.

This is Iwan Robert's shirt from a 2-1 win at Watford on 24 April 2004. It was to be Iwan's last season for the Canaries. His 96 goals for City place him 3rd on the list of the club's all-time top goal scorers.

2004
2005

72 2004/05 DARREN HUCKERBY

2004/05 Darren Huckerby

Darren Huckerby was rightly the Player of the Season for 2004/05 season in the Premier League. He played 36 league games and netted 6 goals during the campaign.

The Canaries were relegated on the last day of the season and, with goal difference, were effectively two points from safety in the final league table.

A late season rally had almost saved City. Home wins over Manchester United, Newcastle United, Charlton Athletic and Birmingham City had put the team in a strong position to avoid the drop.

Frustratingly, winning positions had been surrendered away to Crystal Palace and Southampton, who were both also relegated, in the final few weeks of the season before the last day hammering at Fulham. In fact, City didn't win an away game all season.

2005
2006

74 2005/06 CRAIG FLEMING

2005/06 Craig Fleming

The Canaries played Newcastle United on 26 July 2006 for Craig Fleming's testimonial. Over 15,000 fans watched the Magpies win 2-1 on a night best remembered for a torrential downpour.

Craig Fleming was signed by the Canaries from Oldham Athletic in 1997 for £600,000. The defender would make 382 appearances for Norwich scoring 13 goals. He was Player of the Season in 2003/04 when City won the Division 1 title and he is a Hall of Fame member.

This shirt from the testimonial match was worn by Robert Earnshaw and made by Xara who provided the Norwich kit for 10 seasons from 2001/02 to 2010/11.

2007
2008

2007/08 XX Special Edition

The average attendance at Carrow Road spiked upwards after 2001/02's Play-Off final appearance. With stadium capacity increasing after the re-development of the South Stand in 2004, attendances jumped from an average of 18,629 in 2001/02 to 24,527 in 2007/08.

To celebrate three years where there were over 20,000 season ticket holders, the Canaries produced this one-off shirt. It features the names of season ticket holders and players printed into the fabric of the shirt and the sponsor's logo in gold print.

It was worn for the 5-1 win over Colchester United on 22 March 2008. Jamie Cureton grabbed a hat-trick with Jon Ostemobor and Dion Dublin also scoring.

2008
2009

78   **2008/09** CELEBRATING THE '59ERS

2008/09 Celebrating the '59ers

My Dad watched third division Norwich's 1958/59 cup run. He's still convinced we should have got to Wembley. City beat Ilford, Swindon Town, Manchester United, Cardiff City, Tottenham Hotspur and Sheffield United only to lose to Luton Town in a semi-final replay.

My uncle was in the Police force and got to meet Matt Busby and the Manchester United team before the 3rd round game at Carrow Road. He said they were much too confident and not surprised when they lost.

To mark the 50-year anniversary of that marvellous achievement the club used a one-off strip for their FA Cup ties in 2008/09. Unlike the great 58/59 side, it was to be a very short run in the cup that year. Norwich were beaten 1-0 at home by Charlton Athletic in a 3rd round replay. That game is probably best remembered as manager Glenn Roder's last in charge of the Canaries.

This number 6 shirt was worn by Gary Doherty in both games with black shorts to better match the kit used in 58/59. Doherty played 202 games for Norwich between 2004 and 2010 scoring 12 goals. He's one of few players to have represented the Canaries in the Premier League, Championship and League One. He was Player of the Season in 2005/06.

2009
2010

80 2009/10 DIVISION 1 CHAMPIONS

2009/10 Division 1 Champions

At first, relegation to the third tier for the first time in 49 years was awful. The Canaries had finished a miserable 2008/09 Championship season 3rd from bottom on just 46 points from 46 games. A good 6 points from safety.

The new 2009/10 league season started badly too with an unbelievable 7-1 home defeat to Colchester United, a draw at Exeter City and then another defeat at Brentford.

It took the arrival of new manager Paul Lambert to reverse City's fortunes. His bold, attacking brand of football saw the Canaries charge up the table to win the title with 95 points; 9 points clear of 2nd placed Leeds United.

City's new striker was a big part of that team. Signed from Shrewsbury Town with the help of the fans, Grant Holt would become the first Canary to win the Player of the Year award 3 times. He scored 30 times across all competitors in this promotion season and this is his shirt.

2010
2011

82   2010/11 PROMOTED TO THE PREMIER LEAGUE

2010/11 Promoted to the Premier League

The Canaries followed-up the success of winning Division 1 by finishing second in the Championship in the 2010/11 season.

Paul Lambert's team were hugely enjoyable to watch with a committed group of hard-working players who had a very good habit of scoring very late goals to win games.

Andrew Crofts was typical of the team. He joined from Brighton & Hove Albion in May 2010 and played 68 times scoring 8 goals.

This shirt was worn during a 3-3 draw at Reading on 13 November 2010. It features the special "League One Champions" patch on the sleeves and the Royal British Legion's poppy on the front.

2012
2013

84   2012/13 GRANT HOLT'S LAST GAME

2012/13 Grant Holt's Last Game

The Canaries gave a debut to their new Errea kit for the last game of the season at Manchester City on 19 May 2013.

The hosts had lost to Wigan Athletic in the FA Cup final the week before and their hangover continued as the Canaries won an entertaining game 3-2.

City had secured their top flight status the previous week by thumping West Bromwich Albion 4-0 at Carrow Road. That win along with the 3 points at the Etihad Stadium helped Norwich to finish a very respectable 11th in the table.

Sadly, it turned out to be Grant Holt's last appearance and last goal for City. He left for Wigan Athletic a few months later. It was a great shame to see Holt leave. For a long while, I believed he would go on to get 100 goals for Norwich. His 78 goals in 168 games currently have him 5th on the all-time list of goal scorers.

2012
2013

86 2012/13 FA YOUTH CUP WINNERS

2012/13 FA Youth Cup Winners

Norwich City have won the FA Youth Cup twice; in 1982/83 and again in 2012/13.

The last triumph is perhaps the most remarkable. Since that win, the competition has only been won by bigger and better funded clubs: Chelsea (5 times), Manchester City (2), Liverpool, Manchester United, Aston Villa and West Ham United.

The Canaries beat Chelsea 4-2 over two legs with a team including Josh and Jacob Murphy, Carlton Morris and Harry Tofollo.

This number 11 shirt was prepared but not worn in the final. It features the cup final match print on the front and the autographs of the playing squad on the back.

2014
2015

88   2014/15 CHAMPIONSHIP PLAY-OFF FINAL

2014/15 Championship Play-Off Final

The 2-0 win over Middlesbrough in the Championship Play-Off final on 25 May 2015 was just the most perfect day out for the Canary fans in the 85,656 crowd.

Having enjoyed beating Ipswich Town again in the semi-finals to win through to Wembley, two goals inside 15 minutes put City into a lead that was never seriously threatened. Cameron Jerome and Nathan Redmond become the first Canaries to score at the national stadium.

This is Wes Hoolahan's size "S" Errea made shirt from the final. It features the one-off match details on the front and the Sky Bet Play-Off patches on the sleeves. It has been autographed by the entire squad.

Wes made over 300 appearances for the Canaries scoring 47 goals. He was Player of the Year in 2017 and another one of the small group to have represented City in the Premier League, Championship and League One.

2015
2016

90   2015/16 80 YEARS AT CARROW ROAD

2015/16 80 years at Carrow Road

On 31 August 1935, Norwich City beat West Ham United 4-3 in the first ever competitive match at Carrow Road.

The new stadium had been built in just 82 days after the FA had told the club the old ground at the Nest was no longer suitable for large crowds. A newly built Carrow Road held 35,000 fans. The club declared their new home to be the "eighth wonder of the world".

The 2015/16 season marked the 80-year anniversary of the Canaries move to Carrow Road. To celebrate, West Ham United were invited back for a special pre-season game and the Canaries re-visited the style they had worn back in the 1935/36 season.

This number 10 shirt was worn by Cameron Jerome in that friendly and includes the wonderful "There's no place like home" transfer on the front and "80 years" on each of the numbers on the back.

2017
2018

92   2017/18 JAMES MADDISON

2017/18 James Maddison

Daniel Farke was appointed as City's new manager ahead of the 2017/18 Championship season by Stuart Webber; the club's new Sporting Director.

It was a transformational season for the Canaries as Farke and Webber re-shaped the playing style and squad. Norwich finished the season in 14th but had laid the foundations for the greater successes that were to follow.

A good run in the League Cup saw City exit at Arsenal in the 4th round. The FA Cup run was short but glorious with a 3rd round replay defeat at Chelsea on penalties. The hosts finished extra time with just 9 men after 2 red cards.

This is James Maddison's shirt from the Chelsea game. James was the Player of the Year. He made 49 appearances across all competitors and was top scorer with 15. His outstanding performances earned him a move to Leicester City and an FA Cup winners medal before switching to Tottenham Hotspur. He has also played for England.

2018
2019

94 2018/19 CHAMPIONS AT VILLA PARK

2018/19 Champions at Villa Park

Norwich City won the Championship title on the 5 May 2019, the final day of the 2018/19 season, with a 2-1 win at Aston Villa. It was their 10th win in 14 matches.

The Canaries finished the season with 94 points from 46 games; losing only 6 all season. 4 of those defeats had come in the first 12 games. City had that delightful ability again to score very late goals to win or draw games.

It was the most unexpected of title successes but perhaps the most brilliant so far by a Norwich team at this level.

This is Onel Hernandez's shirt from the title winning game at Villa Park. The popular Cuban was one of the many lovable characters within City's playing squad. He made 43 appearances in all competitions and scored 9 including 2 late, late goals against Nottingham Forest on Boxing Day to help the Canaries to a 3-3 draw.

2019
2020

96 2019/20 FA CUP QUARTER-FINAL

2019/20 FA Cup Quarter-Final

The Canaries reached the FA Cup Quarter-Final for the first time since 1991/92 in the 2019/20 season.

Wins at Preston North End (4-2), Burnley (2-1) and Tottenham Hotspur (4-3 on penalties) earnt City a plum home draw against Manchester United on 27th June 2020.

It would have easily been a sell-out but recently introduced Covid restrictions meant this game was played behind closed doors with no fans present.

Sadly, Norwich lost 2-1 after extra time. This is Ben Godfrey's worn shirt from the game. It features the FA Cup patch on the sleeve as well as additional patches to show support for the NHS and the Black Lives Matter movement.

2020
2021

98   2020/21 TO THE FANS

2020/21 To the Fans

Norwich used this one-off kit design for their 4-1 home win over Reading on 1 May 2020 and this shirt was worn by captain Grant Hanley.

The win secured the Championship title for the Canaries. Promotion had been achieved a few weeks earlier on 17 April 2020 despite a 3-1 home defeat to Bournemouth.

The design of the shirt included a montage of images including the iconic "Welcome to Norwich. A Fine City" sign. Pleasingly, there are none of the usual sponsor logos on the front or back.

The kit was dedicated to the club's supporters who had to follow the team remotely rather than in the stadium for the season. Some of the money from the sale of the limited-edition shirts was then used to support initiatives to improve the atmosphere inside Carrow Road when fans returned to the stadium.

2020
2021

2020/21 TEEMU PUKKI

2020/21 Teemu Pukki

With 88 goals from his City career, Teemu Pukki is the 4th highest goal scorer in Norwich City's history.

He joined on a free from Denmark's Brondby in 2018 and left for Minnesota United in the US in 2023. His 5 seasons with the Canaries were outstanding. He won 2 Championship titles medals and 2 Player of the Year awards.

He scored a Premier League hat-trick against Newcastle United; the first Norwich player to achieve that since Efan Ekoku got 4 goals at Everton in 1993.

He was the EFL Championship Player of the Year and Golden Boot winner in 2018/19. He was in the EFL Championship Team of the Year in 2018/19 and again in 2020/21.

This mud splattered number 22 shirt was worn by Teemu Pukki during the title winning campaign.

2020
2021

102 **2020/21** CHAMPIONS AT OAKWELL

2020/21 Champions at Oakwell

2021/21 was just the weirdest season. Government restrictions for the Covid pandemic meant that most of the games were played behind closed doors. At Carrow Road, just 1,000 fans watched the game against Preston North End. Then 2,000 each for the games against Sheffield Wednesday, Nottingham Forest and Cardiff City.

On the pitch, the Canaries enjoyed a record-breaking season winning the Championship with their highest-ever total of 97 points. They finished 6 points clear of Watford and 10 clear of Brentford who won the play-offs.

This shirt was worn by Grant Hanley in the final game of the season when the Canaries drew 2-2 at Barnsley. Hanley then lifted the Championship trophy; the fifth time the Canaries had won the title at this level.

This was the last of ten seasons where Errea supplied the Norwich kit. They were replaced by Joma for the 2021/22 season.

2022
2023

104   **2022/23** GABRIEL SARA

2022/23 Gabriel Sara

The club crest was re-designed and worn on the team's shirts for the first time in the 2022/23 season. At the time of the re-launch, Sam Jeffery (Commercial Director) said "For the first time in 50 years the club will adopt a newly evolved crest, fit for digital purpose, iconic and most importantly accessible for all".

Whilst it may be more suitable for today, I still miss the charm of the last crest that had served the club so well for such a long time.

This Gabriel Sara shirt shows the new crest as well as a one-off sponsorship for the Mind charity. In a very positive initiative, the club and its main sponsor have donated the shirt sponsorship for one game a season to a local charity for a number of years now.

This shirt was used for the home game against Preston North End on 8 October 2022 which was lost 3-2. However, the skillful Brazilian scored his first goal for the club in this match. In total, he scored 7 from 43 league and cup appearances in the 2022/23 season.

2023
2024

106 **2023/24** NORWICH CITY 1 IPSWICH TOWN 0

2023/24 Norwich City 1 Ipswich Town 0

Ultimately the 2023/24 season finished with a miserable defeat to Leeds United in the play-off semi-final. However, there were still some great games and brilliant moments that will be remembered from this campaign.

For me, the highlight was the 1-0 home win over Ipswich Town on 6 April 2024. A packed stadium, a raucous crowd, a truly wonderful occasion backed-up with a great performance and result. The guy behind me was so happy at the end that he finished up bare chested and twirling his shirt around his head. That's the first time I've ever seen that happen in the City Stand!

15 years indeed Norwich City.

This is Josh Sargent's shirt from that game against Ipswich. Josh had a really good season even with a significant ankle injury that kept him sidelined for 4 months and he finished with 16 goals from 28 matches. Who knows, if he could have played the whole season we may have even finished above you know who in second place.

The hard-working, likeable American had the honour of wearing the famous canary yellow number 9 shirt just like Ron Davies did all those years ago.

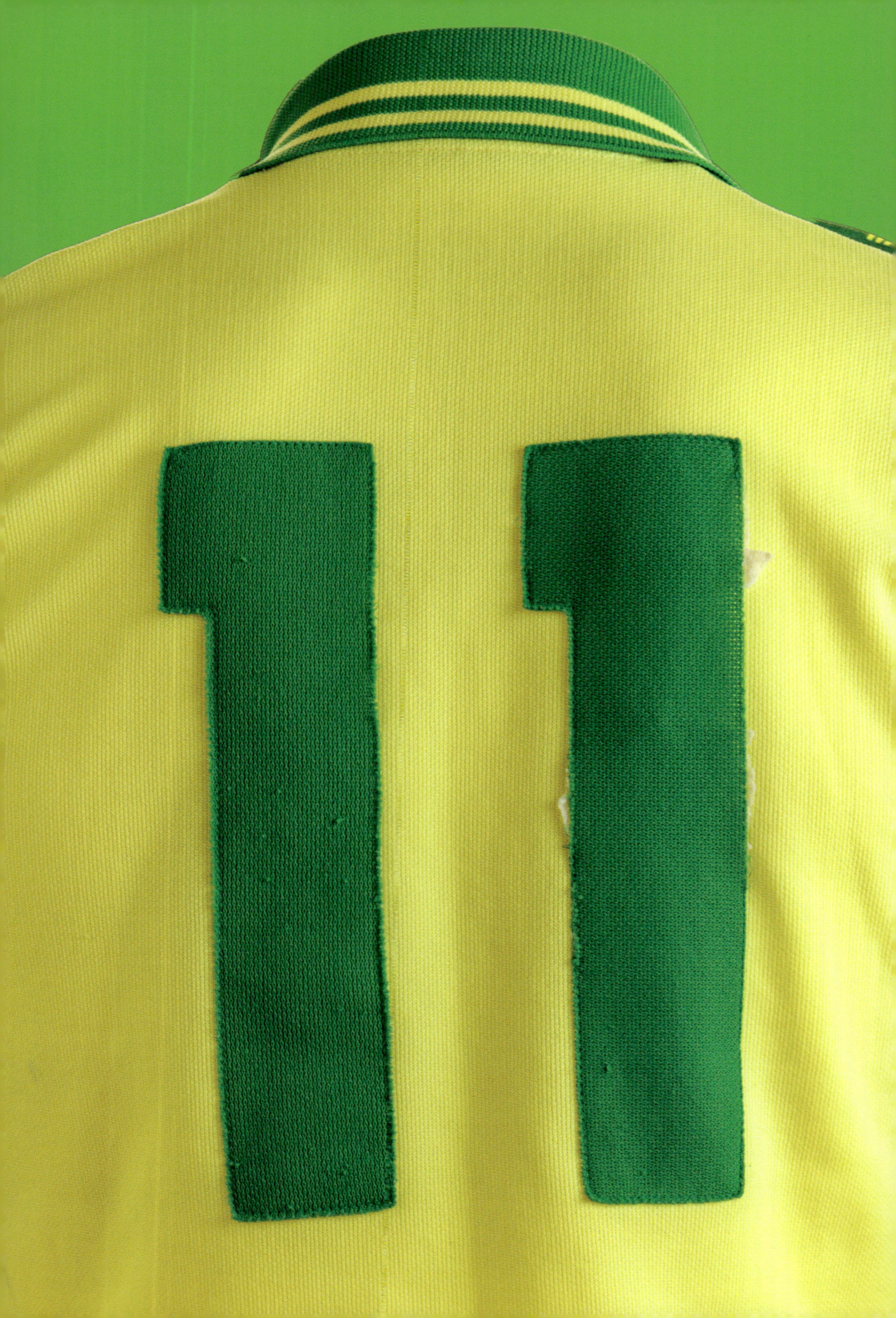
11

Appendix

ABOUT THE AUTHOR

Kevin Goodings is a third generation Norwich City fan. He went to his first game in 1978. He got his first season ticket in 1981. He's old enough now to sit in the City stand and enjoy a hot chocolate at half-time.

Collecting Norwich City memorabilia has been a by-product of supporting the club and over time he has built a small collection of programmes, handbooks and shirts.

You can see much of this at www.ontheballcity.co.uk and contact him via: email to hello@ontheballcity.co.uk.

BILLY POINTER

Billy is a Barlcay season ticket holder with his Dad. They have been there for years and enjoyed some wonderful games and goals together.

Like many other fans, Billy got each new City shirt and before long had a vast selection in his wardrobe. He started looking online for others he didn't have and came across a player's shirt and then the collecting bug really began!

In the last 10 years, he has amassed around 650 shirts from 1971 to the present day. He regularly shares his collection on social media under the name of Norwich Shirts.

NORWICH CITY COMMUNITY SPORTS FOUNDATION

As Norwich City Football Club's official charity partner, the Foundation helps thousands of people every year achieve their goals through sport, supporting some of the most disadvantaged, disabled and talented people across Norfolk. Their vision is to support, inspire, and improve the community.

www.communitysportsfoundation.org.uk

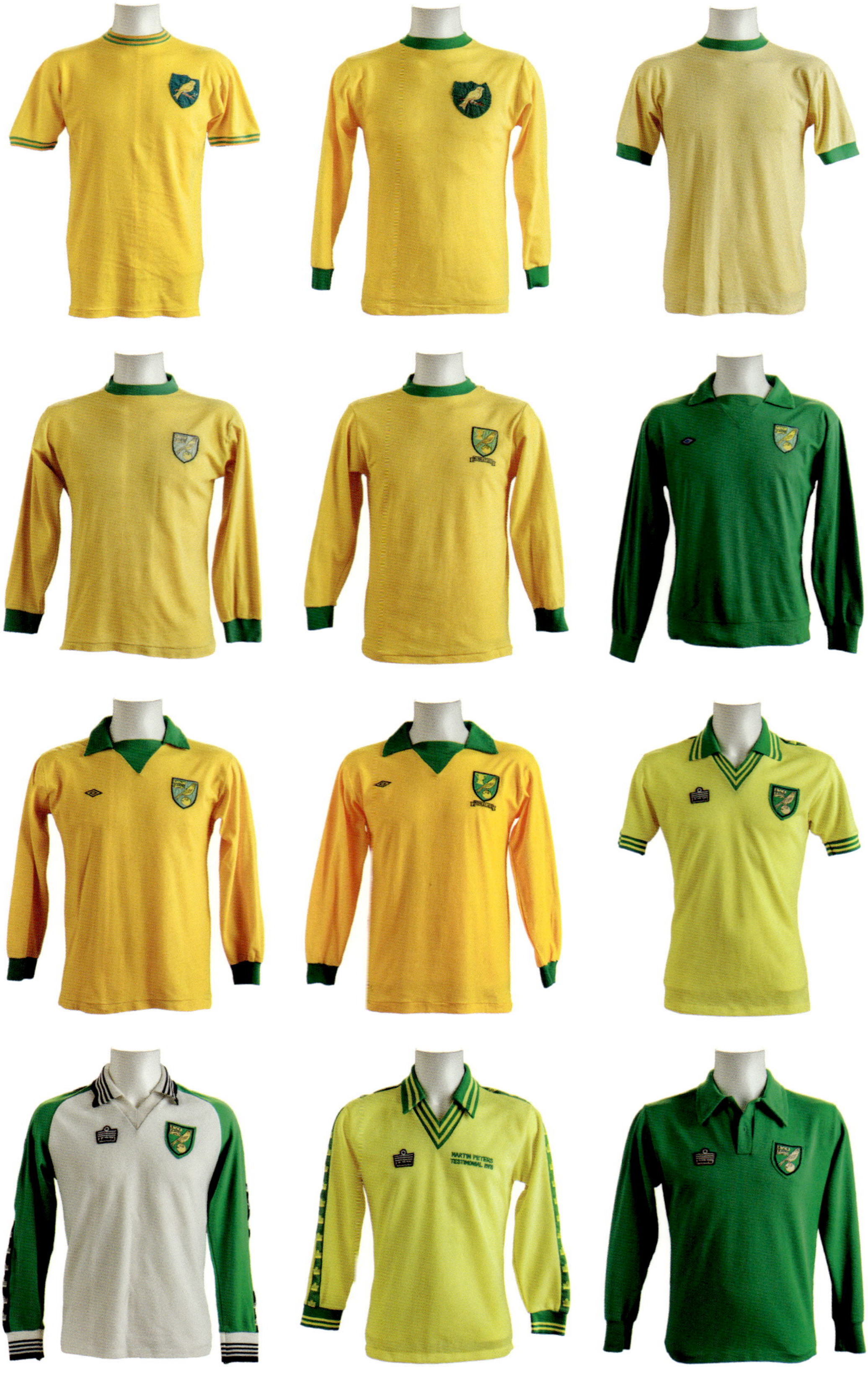
MARTIN PETERS
TESTIMONIAL

Norwich and Peterborough
Mitre
Norwich and Peterborough
Mitre
Norwich and Peterborough
XARA
Digital Phone Company
XARA
Digital Phone Company
XARA
Digital Phone Company
XARA
DPC
Digital Phone Company
XARA
LOTUS
XARA
PROTON
flybe.com
flybe.com

AVIVA
AVIVA
errea
AVIVA
errea
Glen lodge
BAWBURGH GOLF CLUB
errea
AVIVA
errea
AVIVA
errea
LeoVegas
errea
LeoVegas
errea
NHS
dafabet
errea
errea
dafabet
errea
dafabet

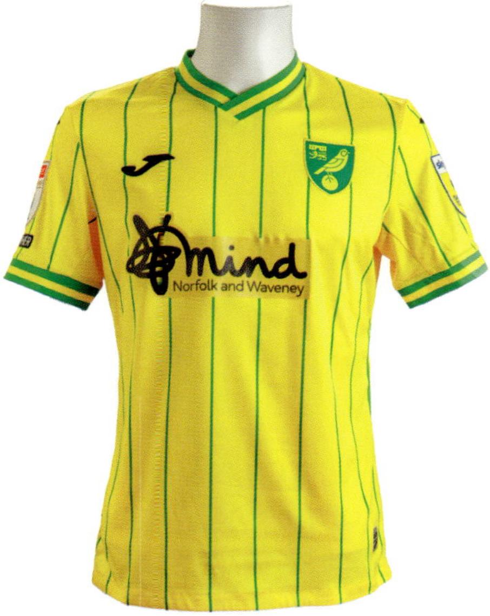
mind
Norfolk and Waveney

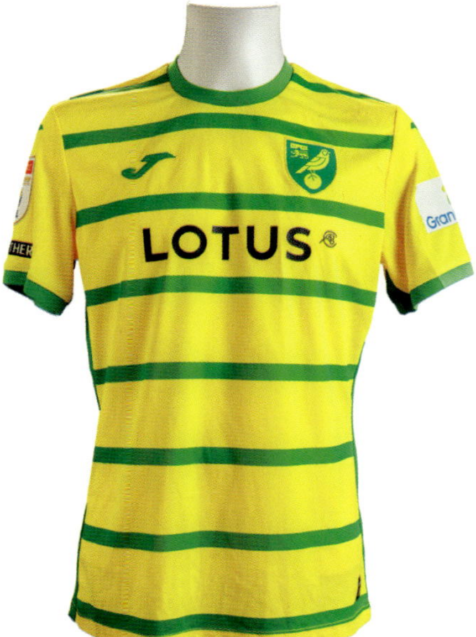
LOTUS